BY MY LAUGH
ITS JEWISH

GW00630707

Also by Harry Blacker
Some of my Best Jokes are Jewish
With Laugh and Affection
Just Like it Was

BY MY LAUGH

ITS JEWISH

NERO
(Harry Blacker)

Foreword by Barnet Litvinoff

VALLENTINE, MITCHELL

Acknowledgements

Despite evidence to the contrary, many of my best friends
are rabbis. It is therefore with particular pleasure that I
record the unfailing kindness and hospitality shown me by
Dow and Fredzia Marmur and Harry (Isaac) Levy and Tonie
whose collection of Nero cartoons seems to exceed my
own.
To my friend Barnet Litvinoff who took time out to write the
Foreword without which this book would be sadly lacking in
merit, a special thank you. Also to old friend Dr Harold
Rose, whose skills with the camera produced the slides I
use to enliven my sundry lectures. To Alfred Hammerson,
Stanley Glazer, Art Director of TV Times and Ian Gardiner
for reprographic assistance. Finally, I raise a glass of kosher
wine to the health of Janus Cohen who unwittingly started
me on the Jewish way of laugh some fifty years ago.

First published in 1982 in Great Britain by
VALLENTINE MITCHELL & CO LTD.
Gainsborough House, Gainsborough Road,
London E11 1RS, England.

and in the United States of America by
VALLENTINE MITCHELL & CO LTD.
c/o Biblio Distribution Centre
81 Adams Drive, P.O. Box 327, Totowa, N.J. 07511

Copyright © 1982 Harry Blacker

ISBN 0 85303 197 5 (Case)

ISBN 0 85303 198 3 (Paper)

Printed in Great Britain by
T. J. Press (Padstow) Ltd
Padstow, Cornwall

To Maidie in loving remembrance
and for the joy and laughter of our grandchildren
Adam, Daniel, Nicola and Carolyn

Foreword

Harry Blacker's ever-widening audience has long been clamouring for a further collection of his cartoons, and at last the demand has been satisfied. What his readers hadn't bargained for, but must receive nevertheless, is yet another Foreword to the volume authored by myself. It is as though I have arranged my perpetual re-election to a seat on the committee, a character perhaps in one of the incidents depicted in the ensuing pages.

However, the true reason for this brief introduction to *By My Laugh, It's Jewish* is that I have become hopelessly entrapped in the Blacker process of creation. I have long been fascinated by the symptoms: his half-feigned nonchalance at the edge of a gesticulating crowd; his sudden withdrawal from a discussion, to draw a line or jot a syllable into his notebook; his ready nod of agreement when an empty argument is voiced; his disarming praise for a pompous lecture, or a boring film, or a pedantic critic. Having learned to suspect his benignity, I am never deceived. His bland expression is but the camouflage employed by an extremely penetrating observer of the communal scene. And when this artist is at work I will know no peace until I have prised from him a set of page-proofs for advance notification of the outcome. Blacker is a demanding man; in return, he extracts a few words from me.

A place in the Jewish hall of fame carries with it its Jewish penalty. Some readers carp at Nero's vulgarity, or his disrespectful view of religion, while others are discomfited because he inundates the sacred cows of

Jewish achievement—a professional career, a stylish marriage—with cascades of ridicule. He bears the stigmata of the stoic waiting in the rain for a late bus after addressing a near-empty hall, having been assured that his mere presence would guarantee a full house. He arrives early for executive meetings of the many organisations that have pressed him into service, and dutifully stays till the end lest he be accused of the disdain with which he punishes such meetings in his art. He is the chosen recipient of interminable pointless stories inflicted upon him by those willing to surrender copyright for what, they are convinced, will make a hugely funny cartoon. This gentlest of men always lends an innocent ear—only when he has a pencil between his fingers does the mischief begin.

Perhaps it is in his wry observation of Jewish family life that he is at his most devastating. This book is the complete antidote to the conventional wisdom which says that all is perfect in that particular department. No reader, on putting the volume down, will be able ever again to regard the peace of the Friday Night scene as anything but a momentary truce in the war between the male aspiration to dominate and the feminine cunning for survival. As Blacker describes it, the love and solidarity which have protected the Jewish family through the vicissitudes of persecution, poverty and affluence will also result in suffocation and a depressing conformism. His comments put us all back where we rightfully belong, among real people with all their faults and virtues, and not a moment too soon.

Well, here we all are, captured in our attitudes of piety and pomposity, and swinging precariously between self-righteousness and self-pity. You will relish every page, and, when the outsider murmurs: 'How odd of God to choose the Jews', you will find here the substance for your retort: 'Oh no it's not. *He* knows what's what!'

Barnet Litvinoff

Every time I feed
the computer a question
on Jewish charities
it answers
'My life I've given
already!'

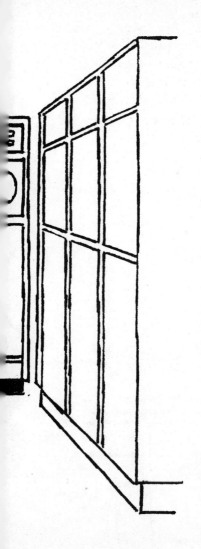

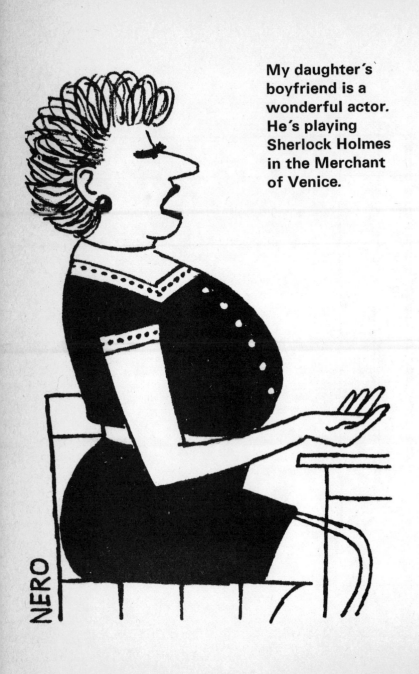

My daughter's boyfriend is a wonderful actor. He's playing Sherlock Holmes in the Merchant of Venice.

For Christ´s sake Moshe, where´s the Chief Rabbi ?

Is this arable land or Israeli?

No Debbie, the 23rd Psalm does not begin 'The Lord is my chauffeur I shall not walk'.

Once upon a time
a lady had an operation
and never mentioned it
to any of her friends.

**Take my advice
and don´t take
my advice!**

May I respectfully remind the choir that
we greet the guest preacher with
Baruch Ha'bah, not Baruch Ha'bore!

The new surgeon at the London Jewish is a real
comedian. He keeps everyone in stitches!

. . . and what gave
you the idea that
I was the Jewish
Welfare Bawd?

Honestly Raymond,
I'm half asleep
already and the rabbi
hasn't even started
his sermon yet.

My Rosser is a bright boy.
He's opened a garage to mend
acupunctures.

Our son was training to be a mohel, but got the push for taking short cuts.

. . . and this gringo
with the ram's horn
asks our Pedro for
a tequila g'doloh!

Married? Of course we´re living in Din!

It's an Israeli watch. It gives the time,
date, month and sidra for the week.

When they told me B.B. was at Hillel House
I naturally assumed it was Brigitte Bardot.
It turned out to be the Bnai Brith.

We now have the name of a reliable accountant
who is willing to join us when he gets out of prison.

I am sorry to announce that our rabbi is only slightly indisposed and will not be with us this evening.

NERO

My Clifford is reading History at Oxford.
My Morrie is reading Maftir at shul.

According to
the shul diary
it's the Omer,
but I wouldn't
count on it.

No, I wasn't mugged. Just jogging without a bra.

Streaker, shmeaker. I´m a rabbetzen
on the way to the mikvah!

Bride and bridegroom, reverend sirs, ladies and gentlemen, pray silence from the bride's father.

**Business is so bad that even the people
who don't pay have stopped coming.**

NERO

. . . and when this tourist asked for the Wailing
Wall, I sent him to the Tax assessment office.

HE prescribed these tablets for the National Health!

NERO

I do believe this is your old bag, Mr Lot!

Once upon a time a man
was asked to propose a toast at a
wedding, but said he was
unaccustomed to
public speaking and didn't!

Suddenly you're a music expert and tell everybody you saw Mozart last week on a 25 bus in Fleet Street. You know the 25 doesn't go down Fleet Street.

Not only are the majority of our children illiterate, but many of them cannot read or write!

My uncle ordered
a white Rolls-Royce
but they delivered
a purple one.
As I said to him,
'Beggars can´t be
choosers!'

Honestly father. Sometimes you get on my tzitzis!

Here´s a job for
our Morrie.
Accountant seeks
qualified assistant.
Honesty no handicap.

My neighbour is such a snob. She says her 3
year old son already knows the 'aloof' beth.

If you're a mohel and not a watchmaker, why have you got a big clock over the shop?
So tell me, mister, what should I put there?

No Patricia.
'Gay in drerd´ is
not Yiddish
for a homosexual
funeral!

Once upon a time
there was a rabbi who
said 'I was wrong'.

Congratulations vicar. It´s a goy!

. . . and wipe
those ruddy smiles
off your faces!

... and what has daddy's little angel been doing today?

Darling! I´ve just laid an oneg.

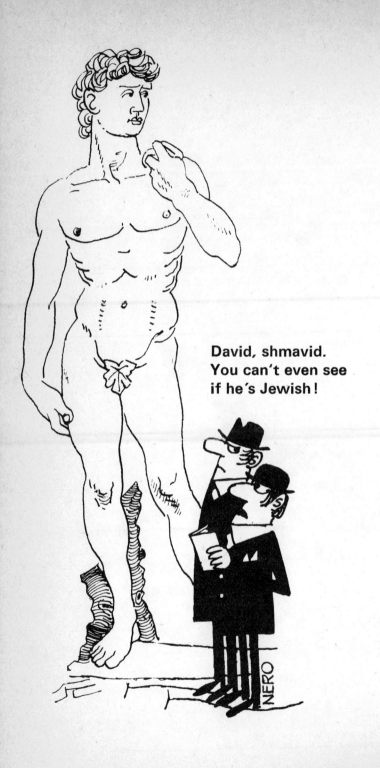

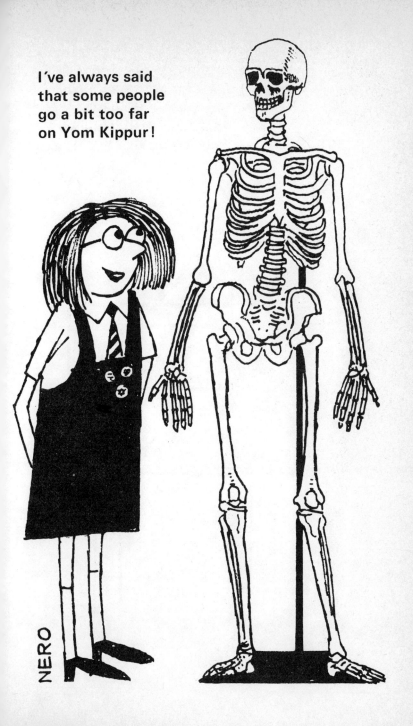

Last year we went round the world on our vacation.
This year, please God, we're going some other place!

Hymie! What's the French for au revoir?

Am I Jewish?
Believe me, I've
got tsoris enough
already!

What's a matter, you can't read English?

**Funny woman
this patient of mine.
Made ME sign a
Covenant for the
Hebrew University
before I could
begin to operate
on her!**

I'm looking for a one-armed solicitor. Every
time I ask my present man for advice he gives it
and immediately says 'But on the other hand...'

You think our cantor emulated himself today? Definitely not. He always sings in a high voice!

Once upon a time
a man told a friend
a joke who hadn't
heard it already!

My Sid is working
in a tallis factory.
The pay is good
and he also gets
fringe benefits.

There seems to be
a slight misunderstanding.
We are actually looking
for Falashas!

I´ve only been unfaithful to
my Sammy twice. Once with
his partner and once with the
Israeli Philharmonic Orchestra!

Rabbi Akiba of Gateshead yeshiva passed on three questions. The answers are as follows. There were Ten Commandments, five Books of Moses and unleavened bread is called motza!

I know it´s traditionally
a stork, vicar, but
Jews use pigeons
and call it
'Pigeon ha´ben!'

Your honour. In view
of the unpleasant nature
of this case, we the jury
by a majority vote have
decided not to mix in.

He´s the sort of
rabbi whose
Yom Kippur sermons
would drive you
to food!

For kosher wine like this they should change the b'rachah to 'Borai pree ha'coffin!

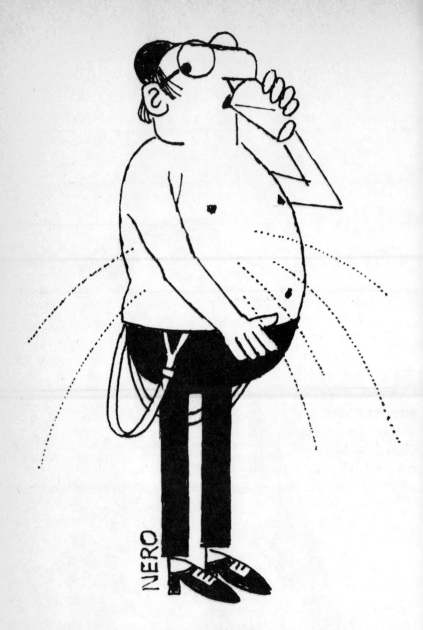

Darling, I think it's time I stopped the treatment at the acupuncture clinic!

. . . and by a clear majority of twelve to four
the Board of Management wishes our rabbi
a speedy recovery from his present illness.

I´ve always said
that if the Sabbath
was on a weekday
more people
would go to shul!

Hymie, mother's decided she'd like to be cremated.
Good. Tell her to get ready and I'll be over
first thing tomorrow morning!

You know, Cecil,
I think death
is Nature's way
of telling us
to slow down!

We've got the Chief Rabbi coming to lunch so
Her Majesty wants you to nip down to Grodzinski
for a cholla, put a mezuzah on the main gate
and change the royal crest to 'Jew et mon droit!'

Get a kosher catering licence and this would be a lovely place for weddings and barmitzvahs!

Tell me rabbi. Is it a sin to play bridge on the
Sabbath?
My dear friend, the way you play it's a sin on any
day of the week!

. . . and this is from a man
who booked an Anonymous
page in our brochure.
He's now complaining
that the word
'Anonymous' should
have been set
in larger type!

It's not serious officer. Just the hot air in
our rabbi's sermon set off the sprinkler system.

They've either chosen
a new Chief Rabbi,
or the Dayan's chimney
is on fire.

I have to go
to my solicitor
to swear an
effing David!

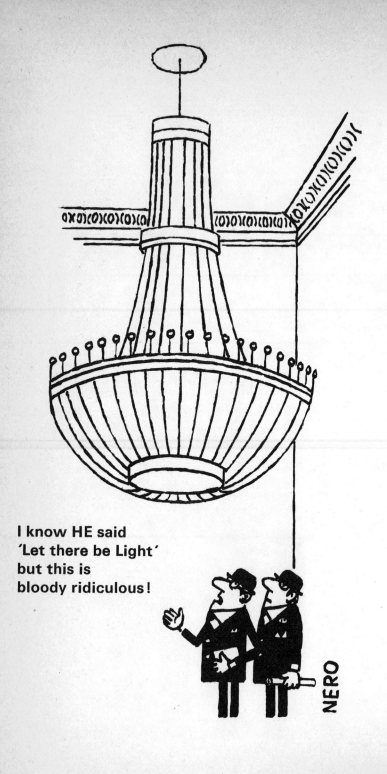

As we´re going
metric, should I
change Miles name
by deed-poll to
Kilometres?

Big deal! So they
bugged an office at
Watergate. In Aldgate
we had bugs in all
the rooms!

Its Booba Job Week
so I´m going to
help my grandmother.

I don't know what mitzvah you've got. Mine
seems to be washing the rabbi's car on Sunday
morning.

Once upon a time during
a research project into Synagogue
Attendance, 80% of those
interviewed said, whenever
they went to synagogue, the
service always seemed to be
Kol Nidre.

. . . and then he said 'Let he who is without sin among you cast the first stone.' I don't think he realised this was a Lubovitch community.

What's the time Moshe?
Now?
When then?

It's Elijah just up from the annual Seder Sip-in and driving drunk in charge of his flaming chariot!

I don´t think these high rise flats will ever catch on !

When we last met at
the 12 Hours for Israel
Exhibition, didn´t I say
we would meet again
on a simcha!

Slalom Aleichem!

This isn't a job
for a Jewish girl.
Perhaps you can
introduce me to a
nice Jewish boy—
but he shouldn't be
a Fairy!